The Library of Living and Working in Colonial Times™

A Day in the Life of a Colonial Blacksmith

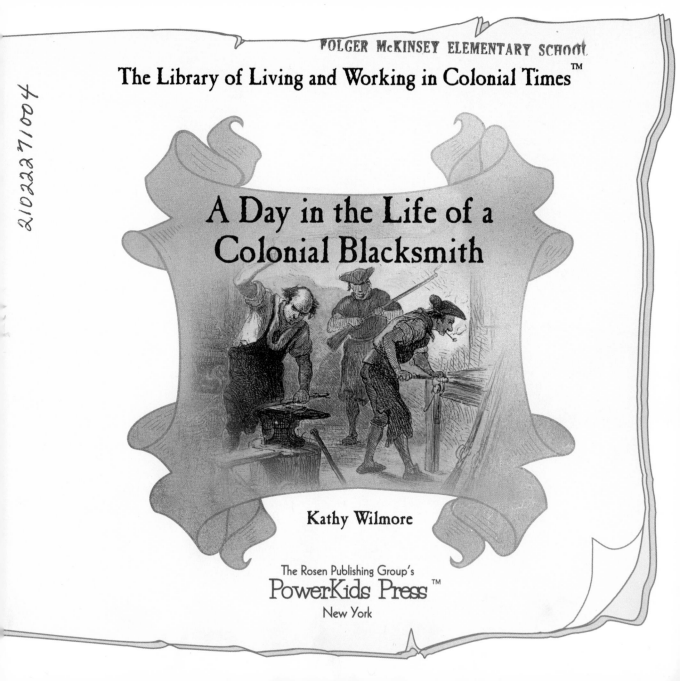

Kathy Wilmore

The Rosen Publishing Group's
PowerKids Press™
New York

To Bryan Brown, for the encouragement, humor, and grace that helped so much as I wrote this book—and to my mother, Julia C. Wilmore, who got me started.

Published in 2000 by The Rosen Publishing Group, Inc.
29 East 21st Street, New York, NY 10010

First Edition

Book design: Danielle Primiceri

Photo Credits:Cover/title p. © The Granger Collection, New York; p. 4 © 1995 North Wind Pictures; p. 7 © Giraudon/Art Resource, NY; p. 8 © Image Select/Art Resource, NY; p. 11 © 1993 North Wind Pictures; pp. 12, 15, 16, 19, 20 © 1999 North Wind Pictures.

Wilmore, Kathy.
A day in the life of a Colonial blacksmith / Kathy Wilmore.
    p. cm. — (The Library of living and working in Colonial times)
Includes index.
Summary: Describes the life of a blacksmith in Colonial Maryland, including his daily work, some of the many things he made, and his importance to the town in which he worked.
    ISBN 0-8239-5425-0 (library binding)
1. Blacksmithing—United States—History—18th century—Juvenile literature. 2. Blacksmiths—United States—History—18th century—Juvenile literature. [1. Blacksmithing—History. 2. Blacksmiths.] I. Title. II. Series.
TT220.W53 1999
682'.0973'09034.—DC21   98-52510
                                                                                           CIP
                                                                                            AC

Josef Braun, his family, his shop, and the other characters are fictional, but the details in this story about Colonial blacksmiths and Colonial life are true.

Contents

Colonial America

In the early 1600s, **colonists** came to America from England and other parts of Europe to start a new life in a new land. They came to farm or find other work. Some workers had skills that made them welcome everywhere. Blacksmiths were always needed to make and repair tools. It took the right mix of skilled workers for a small town to grow. By 1776, the **colonies** had grown and changed and were ready to become **independent** from England. This time before independence is known as Colonial America.

◀ *Many English colonists came to America in the early 1600s searching for a new life.*

A New Trade

Like other colonists, Josef Braun and his family came to the colonies from Europe. They settled in a large port city on the East Coast. Josef's father worked different jobs to support the family. Josef's mother did laundry for wealthy families.

Josef, like many Colonial boys, became an **apprentice** at age ten. He worked for a blacksmtih. Blacksmiths worked with iron, shaping it into tools and other useful items. Josef learned a lot so that he could become a master blacksmith.

A blacksmith and his apprentices at work. ▶

Prized Workers

Blacksmiths were among the most prized **craftsmen**. No **community** could survive without at least one good blacksmith. Farmers and tradesmen needed blacksmiths to make and mend their tools. Everyone needed shoes for their horses and oxen.

When Josef Braun was ready to go into business for himself, he had no trouble finding work. He moved to a small town in Maryland. He opened his own shop and hired a young apprentice named Cy.

◀ Blacksmiths used many tools to help them hold and shape hot metal.

A Popular Spot

A blacksmith's shop was a busy place. Sooner or later, everyone in town was Mr. Braun's **customer**. One busy morning, a customer arrived on horseback from his farm. He had broken his plow and needed Mr. Braun to fix the blade. Another customer needed a new **axle** for his wagon. Mr. Braun's friend Rose had a hole in her teakettle. A young couple was building a new house. They wanted **hinges** made for their doors.

Blacksmiths never ran short of customers. ▶

The Smithy's Forge

Blacksmiths usually worked in a big, open room. It had a huge fireplace called a **forge**, with plenty of charcoal to burn in it. A huge bellows hung nearby. A bellows was used to pump air into the fire to make it burn hotter. There was a big barrel of water and a long counter lined with hammers and other tools. Iron bars hung on the walls. In the center of the room stood the anvil, a big, heavy block of metal that the blacksmith used in shaping the iron.

◀ *A blacksmith with his two main tools, a hammer and an anvil.*

Heating Up

A blacksmith shaped iron by heating it until it was soft. Then he pounded it into the shape that he wanted. It took great strength to lift and hammer the heavy chunks of iron. It also took great skill. Mr. Braun had to heat the iron just right. If it was too cool, it might crack or break. If it was too hot, it would be too soft to shape the way he wanted.

It was an apprentice's job to keep the fire hot. Cy added charcoal when needed and pumped the big bellows to fan the flames.

This smithy is heating metal while his ▶
apprentice pumps the bellows.

Making Repairs

While Mr. Braun's apprentice pumped the bellows, the busy blacksmith used a pair of **tongs** to hold the farmer's cracked plow blade in the fire. He kept turning it to heat the metal evenly. When it was red-hot, Mr. Braun dunked it in the water barrel to cool it. That made a big hiss of steam! Quickly, he pounded the metal to seal the crack.

Next, Mr. Braun melted a little lump of iron in a stone bowl. He poured it over the hole in Rose's teakettle. As it cooled, he hammered it smooth.

◀ *Blacksmiths made a wide variety of objects, large and small.*

Jack-of-All-Trades

By heating and hammering and heating and hammering, a blacksmith could make a lot of things. Like other blacksmiths, Mr. Braun made pots, pans, knives, and forks. He made fences, gates, and railings. He made hooks and latches, lamps and candlesticks. He made metal rims for wagon wheels and anchors for ships. He made weather vanes for the tops of barns. Some days, all he did was make nails. A good Colonial blacksmith could make 3,000 nails in one day!

A blacksmith making nails for horseshoes. ▶

Shoe Business

Like many blacksmiths, Mr. Braun was too busy with other tasks to shoe horses. He made horseshoes but left the work of putting them on the animals to a **farrier**. Mr. Braun worked with a farrier named Ben.

Shoeing horses was fairly easy, but Ben needed a special machine to shoe oxen. Mr. Braun and Cy helped Ben get the ox into straps, then they turned a wheel to lift the ox off the ground. With the ox raised, Ben could reach the bottom of the ox's hooves and nail on the shoes.

◄ *One of a blacksmith's regular jobs was making shoes for horses and oxen.*

Day's End

When evening came, Mr. Braun closed the shop. He oiled his tools to keep them from rusting. Cy cleaned out the forge, so it would be ready to light the next morning.

Mr. Braun studied the book he used to keep track of his customers' orders. He saw that he had plenty more work to do the next day!

Web Sites:

http://www.e-market.net/villageoaks/smith.htm
http://www.slic.com/bigelow/bsmith.htm

Glossary

apprentice (uh-PREN-tis) A young person learning a skill or trade.

axle (AK-sul) The rod that connects two opposite wheels, as on a car or wagon.

colonist (KAH-luh-nist) A person who lives in a colony.

colony (KAH-luh-nee) An area in a new land where a large number of people move, but remain under the rule of their old country.

community (kuh-MYOO-nuh-tee) A group of people living in the same neighborhood or town.

craftsman (KRAFS-mun) A worker with special skills, especially one who works with his hands.

customer (KUS-tuh-mer) A person who buys goods or services.

farrier (FAR-ee-ur) A person who puts horseshoes on horses' and oxen's hooves.

forge (FORJ) A furnace where metal is heated.

hinge (HINJ) A device that connects two objects (such as a door and a wall) so that one can swing back and forth.

independent (in-dih-PEN-dent) To be free from the control, support, or help of others.

tongs (TONGZ) A tool used to grab and move objects that are too hot or too cold to touch.

Index